Words Unspoken

MADALINA COMAN

A COLLECTION OF POETRY AND POETIC PROSE

WORDS UNSPOKEN
WRITTEN AND ARRANGED BY MADALINA
COMAN

www.instagram.com/madalinacoman

www.facebook.com/madalina.poetry

www.twitter.com/mada_c

Cover Illustration by Beatriz Mutelet
Interior Illustrations by Beatriz Mutelet

www.instagram.com/beatriz_mutelet

Cover Design by Mitch Green
Interior Design by Mitch Green

www.instagram.com/mitch_grn

Humans are built, not made.
Our experiences, and our history,
have a say in who we are, and what we
become, but it is our choices that matter
most in the end.

The more we fight to have a voice
in our own becoming,
and the more responsibility we take
in our reshaping,
the more fulfilling the journey
of self-discovery
and rebirth.

Words Unspoken was written to speak to our
hearts, our minds and our souls about the
immense capacity humans have for resilience
and survival, for becoming and flourishing
after having been broken to pieces.

Dedication

This book is a dedication to all you beautiful humans – the ones who look at their broken hearts and wonder whether they are enough, whether they will ever be enough and whether they will ever be able to love again; the ones who have lost a part of themselves while loving and breaking and now doubt they'll ever be whole again.

For my father – for showing me the negative effects of having to keep my mouth shut while he was alive & also for giving me the power to finally find my own voice through his death – I love you and I forgive you.
Rest in peace. I will always miss you and I hope your spirit knows how much I mean it.

For my grandmother – without you, there would be no book, because I would have no self. Thank you for showing me what unconditional love looks and feels like. Thank you for sacrificing your youth to raise me. This book is as much mine, as it is yours. I love you!
Te iubesc!

Preface

Words Unspoken is a story of love, heartbreak, loss, healing and becoming, carefully curated in the form of free-verse poems, quotes and short-prose that aim to reveal the different emotions felt on my writing journey.

Growing up, I often felt the need to keep quiet for various reasons: fear of getting in trouble at home with my father, fear of being bullied, ridiculed, shamed at school; fear of being rejected in relationships for showing too much or too little love, and the list can go on.

This year, my father passed away and this experience made me realize the need to find my voice again. I started writing about the grief experienced after his death and my forgiveness process, only to realize that there were so many other places in my heart silently crying to be heard, noticed and given a chance to heal.

This book is aimed at empowering you to claim your voice back after feeling shattered; it is about claiming your power back and starting to believe in yourself again after having your heart broken; it is about changing the narrative of your life and who you see yourself as capable of becoming.

When you swallow your words for too long, you begin to believe your words don't mean much. You end up thinking what you have to say is not worth sharing and that you will not be able to contribute much to conversations in relationships. And before you know it, an inability of expression will soon enough lead to issues of self-esteem.

We were not born to be silenced. We need to stand up for the words in our hearts. We need to give them a voice and let them be louder and louder every day, until we start recognizing ourselves again.

There were far too many words hidden in my heart and begging to see the light of day; far too many words that were dying a slow and painful death on the tip of my tongue out of fear of being judged for feeling, breaking and loving. The moment I realized that maybe I was not the only one feeling these things, was the moment I gathered enough courage to talk openly about the truth in my heart. And all in hopes that someone else who might be reading them and finding himself/herself in those same situations, might benefit from my experience in some shape or form.

The main reason I write my pieces in lower case letters and only capitalize the word "I" is to give it the most importance. You are important. You are worth it. What you have to say is worth it. Your voice is worth it. Your "I" *is of value.*

My hope is that together, we can begin to breathe life, love and healing back into your life, but before we begin, you need to remember that this journey was my journey. You are now in the passenger seat. There will be times when my journey will not resonate with yours;

in those moments, I want you to remember that we all have different healing paths. We all break and heal a little differently.

Healing is not linear and you should never feel as if you are on a schedule. Do things in our own time and respect your journey of healing. No amount of time is the right amount of time. There is no destination to be reached. *This is a process and the destination is the journey.*

Thank you for giving me the chance to walk you through my journey. I hope you enjoy my words, for they were put together with a lot of love and care. I am entrusting you with a piece of my heart – be gentle with it, while also being gentle with yourself.

Yours, in eternal gratitude,
Madalina

don't let unspoken words
make a permanent home
in the back of your throat.
you shouldn't get used
to staying silent
when
all your heart wants to do
is scream.

The Love

You are embedded within me. You've seeped through every layer, every fiber of my being and carefully nestled the fragrance of your memories in the deepest core of my soul. By your side, I am lost in a trance; completely intoxicated with all that you are. I walk around drunker than after a shot of whiskey, carrying your wild in a secluded corner of my heart, just in case. Just in case one day, you decide to become more than just a memory. Just in case my heart begins to swell up again with the immensity that was you. And I still tremble at the thought of you when the moon whispers back your name in the middle of the night like a sweet lullaby.

Just when I think I am rid of you for good, something irresistible deep inside of me brings me back to you; it is as if your heart calls back for me and the more I fight the temptation to return, the more I lose sleep, I toss and I turn. And suddenly I miss you like hell, when mere moments ago you barely existed and now I am bursting with cravings for more. You pulse through my veins; erupt in my brain and I forget it's winter. My heart no longer feels as if it needs to wilt. Spring is restored and I don't care anymore: not if I die tonight from all this love inundating me like ecstasy; not if I burn to ashes again as I inhale the tone of your voice and let your fingers trace down my spine and make velvet out of my thighs; not if this dangerous dance in the silence of the night takes me away from reality.

I'd make the sun fall from the sky, if I knew
we could love each other just one more time.

let me

fall

like

a summer rain

on your skin.

the loves
we cannot write about,
the ones
we cannot put into words,
those are the loves that
stay with us
forever.

sometimes,
we don't even know
something is missing
from our lives, until
we meet someone
who makes us

feel complete.

every woman

who has ever

loved

with her whole being,

has stardust

stuck

in the cracks

of her heart.

learn to love her,
the way she needs
to be loved,
rather than the way,
it comes easy

for you to love.

I lived
a thousand lives
in just
a few moments
with you.
they are all
on repeat,
every night
in my dreams.

every drop of you,
reminds me of
my favorite wine.
crisp and fresh,
with a bit of a zingy quality
showing off your acidity.
your texture –
smooth and velvety,
the perfect balance
of everything I yearn for
and can never get enough of.
but what makes you – you
is

the long finish,
that lingers in my mouth
years after having
tasted you.

your lips melted
all my words away.
now,

even silence
tastes like you.

I spilled my love
into you
because
my heart was overflowing.

these arms,
were never meant
to just be filled with flesh.
these arms,
were meant to catch you
every time you fell.
these arms,
were meant to hold you
like you had never been held before.
these arms,
were meant to support you
no matter the struggle.

these arms,
were never meant
to be empty of you.

I loved him
even when
he didn't
(know he loved me)

you might not see it now,
but, I rest in
the book I gave you for valentine's day,
the streets we used to tread
before and after lunch –
hopelessly looking for a reason
to steal just one more minute
out of each other.
I rest in
the hours we spent
in your unmade bed,
your fingers playing with my hair,
the faint whispers we shared
as our breaths collided before
surrendering to each other again.
I rest in
everything you wish you had said,
but never had the courage to.
and I'll rest here, dormant,
until the day,
you start feeling me, too.

who
he was,
was nothing
compared to

who he was with me.

his eyes told stories
his heart
knew nothing about.

all I ever wanted,
was to feed your soul
so much love,
that it never had to find out,
what it's like,
to go to bed hungry.

I am going to
go back in time
and love you
so that
I don't suffocate our present
with my intensity.

and I miss you
the most
when I try
not to miss you
at all.

my favorite
memories of you
are the moments
I knew I was going to miss
even before
they were gone
and became
memories.

this morning,
I am not in my skin.
I am back to a time
when you and I
were possible.
loving you,
not with my words,
but with the heat
of my breath.
filling your lungs up
with more of me
than they've ever
thought themselves
capable of carrying.
so that for once
you are fuller of me,
than I ever was
of you.

I know it was real,
because I felt it in my bones,
under my skin,
and in every hidden crevice
of my heart.
and I wish,
someone had taken a photo of your eyes
as they were falling in love with me, too.
and then, maybe
just maybe,

you would have believed
it was real, too.

there is love and then, there is true love.

this inescapable force you have no time to make preparations for. it envelopes you suddenly, effortlessly, and doesn't follow any rules. you can't predict its devastating effects and you don't see it coming so you can avoid it. and the moment you put expectations on love is the moment it starts losing its magic. this type of love needs to breathe. the more you try to control it, the more it shows you it's had you since the beginning. you can't fight what you don't see coming. and when you realize its power, it is already too late. you are buried so deep in it and sinking deeper and deeper by the day. there are no antidotes. no shortcuts. no exit signs. no maps to show you a way out without tearing you to pieces.

true love requires tremendous courage and maybe that is why it doesn't show itself to everyone.

every night,

as the moon rises

and darkness falls,

I write your name

in the sands

of my heart,

only for the waves

of tomorrow

to sweep it away

with the first rays

of sunlight.

he passed through life
like the whisper
of water,

he passed through me
like hunger.

in the folds of your skin,
in the depth of the universe,
that was your mind,
in the fire of your breath,
in the hidden corners of what I thought
was your heart,
I found answers

that lied beautifully
and tasted
as sweetly as honey.

you avoid men
like your father,
your entire life.
only to end up falling
for one just like him.
see, in the process of
running from what
scared you about him,
you forgot he was not
only made of flaws.
he was also made of charm,
warm smiles and gentle eyes.

no wonder this new guy
feels so strangely familiar.

I can never bury
my love for you
deep enough
for it to stop finding
its way back
into the light.
the more I try,
the harder
it bounces back

like a boomerang.

you're like my favorite book.
I can never put you down
for good.
I always come back
for a second,
and a third,
and a fourth read.
a never-ending game
of cravings for more.
I know unless
I burn this book
and all the stories inside,

I'll always crave just
one last read out of it.

I sway back and forth
like the pendulum
in my grandmother's home

between keeping you
and letting you go.

the more I try
to block you out of my mind,
the more,

my mind
invites you in.

I wasn't yours to have
　　and you,
　　weren't mine to lose.
　　but you,
　　had me anyway
　　and I,
　　lost you all the same.

my heart beating
thousands of miles away
from my chest.
as if
I had died and someone
had saved my heart
just in time,
to transplant it
into another body.
it is still alive somewhere, beating.

...although, not where I am,
but where you are.

you were expecting me
to arrive in a box,
wrapped up in tissue
and with a bow on top.

I came dressed
in vulnerability,
while you were looking
for my layers.

-there never were any,
with you

when the clothes
and our masks
come off
and we're forced to be
authentically,
and unapologetically
ourselves –
that's when I feel most comfortable.
looking at you
and feeling your skin pressed against mine,
sensing your soul
trying to come out of your body
and merge with mine –
that's when my whole being
screams for you.
a tango of our bodies
breathes life into the room
and feeds the flames of our love.
a dance known solely by our hearts,
unseen and unheard,
invisible to the world,
but tangible in our memories...

and those are the moments I want to relive...

somehow,
we kept finding each other,
no matter how many times
the earth went around the sun.

for a second there,
it felt as though,
we had been predestined
to be together.

for a second...

like a magic wand,
you used your smile
to make a home
out of my heart,

even though,
you never meant
to stay.

you showed me what love
could look and feel like,
until I surrendered
my heart to you.
whole.
you thought our attraction
was a distraction.
and so,
you blindsided me
with your silence.
you left me wondering
what I had done wrong.
you left me starving
for answers,

just to show me that you could.

I never
wanted to stop
having firsts
with you,

but,
somehow
lasts were
more your thing.

my heart
has hardened,
with every broken promise
that you've made.
only to be softened,
with your every kiss
in all the places
that once hurt.

I've been trying
to forget you,
yet,

I can't even bring myself
to regret you.

someone once asked me how I knew that you'd come back. I always knew because of what I gave to you. it was raw. pure. genuine. it was true. people don't walk around willing to give their hearts out to others like that. unconditionally. when your heart feels what it is like to be set on fire in a split second. to feel flutters of wings. slow dances of ecstasy. waves of infinite warmth and insanity of thought and feeling. on the spot. no heart can ever resist the call to come back.

this has never been a question of "if";
it has always been a matter of "when".

when
you least expect it,
I'll pop up.

first,
as a splash of green
in your winter.
then,
as a quiet hum
in your solitude.
and,
before you know it,
you'll be wondering

why you ever let me go.

one day,

your mind will let go of me.

you'll go on with your life,

the way the sky and the air

go on after a summer rain.

and then one day,

as you're gazing into your new lover's eyes

and she's tracing her fingers

down your chest,

your body will remember me.

because while the mind can forget,

the body always remembers.

just the way,

the soil never forgets

the blessing of rain

in the middle of a scorching summer day.

I leave drops of my unwavering love for you suspended on leaves, getting ready to drop at the right time. I imagine them falling as you unknowingly walk underneath them. or fall onto the ground and nourish it so that flowers sprout everywhere your feet step. you'll see me in magnolias smiling down on you as you take a morning run. you'll feel my passion in red roses and tulips pulling your lips close enough to touch their petals. your nostrils will remember my scent the moment you approach a lilac in bloom in early spring and the cherry blossoms will take you on trips down memory lane you wish you had forgotten about. you'll die a little every time you look at all this beauty. this passion. this blooming. and remember the strength of the woman who loved you, even though you were not ready to love her. because loving in this manner requires of a heart what is needed of a flower to break through concrete. and live. and thrive. and bloom, in spite of it all.

and where will you ever find
another love like that again?

The Hurt

They say feelings are our teachers; they are only meant to stay until they are done teaching us the lessons we are meant to learn. And so, I let myself feel. I let all this pain sink in.

I have been trying to dig myself out of the ruble you left me buried under for so long. I find myself more dead than alive, but I let myself burn; burn to ashes in hopes of some grand rebirth following. You left while rivers of my tears were still pouring down my face. I was kneeling down begging you for another chance and you never once even bothered to look back. You fed me to the wolves willingly and unremorsefully. Depression took its first bite at my throat. My voice muffled. I found myself mute and lying in a bath of bloody feelings I did not know what to do with. How do you put into words the unimaginable? How do you find the words to explain to your heart some people might never come back? Suddenly, the garden of my heart, full of beautiful roses and delicate azaleas is all black water and ashes. There is nobody to tend to it anymore. Nobody to grow its flowers for. I am drowning deeper and deeper into the darkness with no way out, no crevice to hide in just for a little while, until I regain an ounce of strength back to continue fighting. No! This pain never stops and there is no one to tell about it as I rapidly lose myself in it. All that's left of us are stories and memories crushing me. When did we become mere strangers to one another?

I am left with no other choice, but to embrace the shards of what we once had and rearrange this brokenness into something bearable again.

I cannot breathe under the weight of all this pain, but I know one day I will.

I know
how it feels
to be breaking
(again and again)
and needing
a break.

a beautiful german village,
raided by the natzis.
decimated.
ruble and dust is all that remains
of a once glorious parade of
fresh fruit markets,
fields of blooming purple flowers,
friendly laughs shared early on sunday mornings,
while reading the newspaper over a cup of coffee.
Lovers treading old brick streets hand in hand,
stealing kisses from each other.
one wonders what cataclysm
might have caused such damage,
such reckless wreckage,

that's what your leaving did to me.

at night,
the sky rains tears
only my pillows
know about.

broken is beautiful

somehow these words sink into my wounds like a scalpel looking to draw blood. I often wonder about the people making such statements. I'd like to sit on the sill of their windows and see how they live. what they experience. what gives them the right to make such statements.

once the brokenness has passed and the wounds become scars, there is beauty, strength and healing in the transformative power of pain. but, while you're in the middle of the storm, there's no beauty in being broken. while you're riding those emotional waves, beauty is the last thing on your mind.

you wake up in the morning and don't notice your legs; you cannot appreciate how special, how unique it is that you have awakened. you cannot acknowledge the privilege of having legs that work and being alive.

with every new sunrise, you're not rising. you're digging a deeper and deeper grave for yourself. you pass by the blooming trees and your eyes, don't see beauty. your heart doesn't think of rebirth. it feels nostalgia for the better days you used to have when everything didn't feel so heavy, so charged and so gloomy. *you blind yourself to what is, because you are stuck in what was and you won't let go of what could have been.*

nighttime comes and you hope. you pray. you beg. that once your head hits the pillow and those tired eyes full of tears close, there will be relief coming your way in the morning. but you know damn well you're lying to yourself again, because there will be no coming out of this in the morning.

you're caught in a circle of suffering that has its claws so tightly anchored in your body, it suffocates you. it drains everything out of you. until there is no more hope left in you and only emptiness to be tasted.

so, don't tell me there's beauty in being broken, because you have not been where I have been. a hand to hold while I battle the waves is all I need in my brokenness. when the light comes, I will see the beauty in everything again, but while I'm still in my darkness, don't talk to me about the light, for my eyes cannot see what cannot be felt and there is no light in my darkness.

*a message for those friends who think they are
helping someone in pain by telling them
the many reasons they have for enjoying life:
talking about light when all one sees around
is darkness, is the fastest way to make that
person feel guilty for their own feelings and
succumb even further into their nothingness. if
you wish to help: be a warm and nonjudgmental
presence while they pour their hearts out to
you. saying nothing in those moments is better
than saying life is beautiful; it might be for you,
but not for them; not yet, at least.*

we sleep off the things that hurt. that inconvenience us. we sleep off headaches, hangovers, stress, sadness and anxiety. but what do we do with the things that we cannot sleep off? what do we do with the things that wait for us to fall asleep so they could haunt us further into our dreams?

what do I do with you?

I went to palo alto today
and set a flower
on the grave
of our love.

left,

before it was too late.

the weight
of the words we shared
is nothing,
compared to the weight
of the words that

die a slow death
every night on my lips
before I close my eyes.

in the deep fires
of heartbreak
I saw the way

a rose dies,
before blooming.

patches
of yellow flowers,
each
reminding me of

the drive to santa cruz
we never took.

absence is alive,

has a pulse of its own,

and it hurts

like hell.

the heaviness of this silence

reminds me of

the heaviness of your shoes

last time they stepped

all over me

mistaking me for a doormat.

look deep
into my sorrows
and find your name
tattooed

on every single piece
that hurts.

I minimize the bad.
I blow the good
out of proportions.
and that's how
I keep myself from
letting you go.
by fooling my heart
into believing that you were
something more

than the coward
that you actually are.

you liked me as a river,
always discovering,
always traveling to
new and exciting places.
you came alive inside of me.
you liked me as a waterfall,
with healing water.
each time you stood under me,
you washed away your past.
my waters cleansed you
of your fears, your shame, your pain.
you came out cleansed and rejuvenated.

you never liked me as a storm.
and I am more a storm
than any other type of water.

if my tears had a voice,
they would

shout rivers of
"I miss you" s.

at night,
is when I need
to fight your shackles
the hardest.

the absence of your words
lives between my ribs,
parting them wide
whenever it rains outside.

how agonizing it is
to watch the droplets merge
with each other,
so effortlessly.

just the way our limbs bent
without ever breaking
in their incessant search
for the most pleasurable position
in which to lose themselves,
intertwined,
under the moonlight.

we were
the best thing that
never happened
to each other.

I tried
to write
the silence for you,

but you never let me
learn your language.

I wanted this
to be love,
but the more I fought
to make it a reality,
the more,

I drowned
in disillusionment.

I fell in love
with an untrue version of him –
a bent reality,
a poor reminder
of the illusion
I dreamt love would be.

write away your pain,
they said.
so,
I started writing
to forget you.
but,

the more I write,
the more I remember you.

our last goodbye –
felt like poison
in my veins.

I slip
into sadness and missing
every night before bed,
as if they were my most comfortable
pieces of clothing.

I had been carrying buckets and buckets of sunshine and happiness from across the street for days. the tall blonde in the red heels always looks so cheery when coming out of her perfectly manicured house and so I figured if I changed the water, I might actually be able to get rid of this emptiness. this missing. this mud stuck in my throat. this numbness, I carry on my hips and in my lower back. on every little place that misses the warmth of your lips. little did I know, happiness, even when in buckets is not enough to fix a broken heart. not before you sit with the sadness first. not before you bathe. you drown in the salt of your tears until every single finger and toe is pruned to perfection. and so, I took the silk robe off, and carefully placed it on the empty stool next to the newly remodeled marble bathtub and submerged myself in warm, pure, sad, loving tears.

you can wait months,
sometimes years,
and flush the drugs
and the alcohol
out of your body.

but,

how do you expect
to get rid of something
that is sewn into your heart
with indestructible
and everlasting thread?

- human connection is the most powerful drug.

of all the lives
in all the universes,
I ended up
in the one

I have to spend
without you.

there will always be
too much of my love
going around
and

*too little of you
appreciating it.*

I've filled your heart
to the brim
with every last drop
of my love,

*if only you had known
what to do with it.*

I can't
keep waiting for you
to wake up
and decide that
you're ready.

you built me up,
only
to start tearing me down
...slowly.

I call it lack of inspiration, but do these words really choose to stay hidden? or are they coming from a place that terrifies me so much that I'd rather just declare them lost?! have you managed to crack open a part of me that I didn't know I had? have you done it again? have you brought the beast out in broad daylight when it was only allowed to roam these streets at night? I see it resting under a big oak tree and imagining all the things she would do to you. unutterable. unthinkable things. the kinds you can't go to the river in the morning and wash off. the kinds that stain. your heart. your mind. the space between your legs. the back of your neck. the kinds you crave at 2:00 a.m. the kinds you go into withdrawal without. the kinds your lips get hungry for and your arms get greedy about. the kinds that consume you slowly, but steadily. the kinds you never forget and always go looking for once the sun is out.

the kinds I don't know how to
give out gracefully. delicately. the
kinds I give out loud.

we never were
much about moderation,
middle grounds or grays.
we were a black or white,
an all or nothing
kind of a deal.
we either burnt with
the intensity of the sun
or froze to death
like the trees and the flowers
in the middle of winter.
so, I guess
it shouldn't be surprising,

we ended up strangers
after having been
the best of friends.

you were buying property
in my head.
while,
I was only permitted
to rent space
in yours.

it wasn't
your no that hurt me
the most.

it was the maybe.

you weaved a crown
of almosts and maybes,
placed it on my head
and convinced me
of how beautiful
I looked with it on.
and here I was,
thinking that maybe
you had given me
a crown
weaved of hope
and blooming daisies.

when it rains on you
with uncertainties,
for long enough
you start mistrusting
the rain.

one morning,
you're taking a shower
and you realize showers
might not be as cleansing
as you once thought, after all.

you take a trip to the beach,
soak your feet
in the warm water at sunset,
but somehow it doesn't feel
as poetic as it once was.

and then,
you take a moment
to wonder when and how
you started mistrusting
something as basic, as pure
and as beautiful as water?

it is in

the *what ifs*

where

I can taste the bitterness

of love

the most.

I put you and our love
on a pedestal.
I made you a god.
I trusted you enough
to put all
my dreams,
my hopes,
my fantasies,
my fears,
and my truths
in the palm of your hand.
and I gave them all to you
as an offering.
without hesitation,
without ever realizing
that the only thing you were
was a devil,
dancing in my pain
and tempting me with everything
I ever wanted and you could have given me,
but chose to steal from underneath me instead.

I've always been bad
at following maps.
I don't know why
I ever led myself to believe
I'd be able to find
my way to your heart.

we slipped,
you and I.
we slipped from
each other's hearts,
the way one slips
on a stubborn bar of soap
when coming out
of the shower
still dripping water.
it was quick and painful,
but it lingered.

it still lingers.

do you ever feel lost?

when I am lost, I have small moments of self-transcendence. I search for everything, from meaning and purpose in my life, to the hands whose touch once made me moan, to the lips that excited even the most obscure and well-hidden of thoughts.

I search for feelings that I miss and I want to relive. I search for his eyes in crowds. I turn around when someone's voice reminds me of his. I jump, startled by the smallest of noises because my awareness of myself is so far removed. I live in my own bubble with no attention paid to the things around me.

when I'm lost, I revert to being a child, learning everything all over again. everything is new and unknown and I am rediscovering things as if I had never experienced them before.

when I am lost. I am not myself. I am a version of myself who wanders the world in search of reuniting with all her other selves lost along the way. in different cities and countries where

she experienced pain. where the hurt pinned
her down with no way out.

when I am lost, I search for all these pieces of
myself scattered everywhere in time and space
and I'm hoping that once I find them, *I can feel
whole again.*

there were quite a few sunrises left in the heart of their love, but he had chosen to turn a blind eye to them all. it was easier for him to run away than to put into words why no matter how much he tried, he couldn't stop thinking about her. he quoted guilt when asked why he left. but she knew better than to be fooled by semantics.

she wasn't going to confuse cowardice with guilt.

what scared you the most,
wasn't seeing my heart
full of love for you.
what made you run away,
was catching a glimpse
of what was starting to bloom
in your own heart.

you talked
about wanting
to travel the world,
and yet,
you were scared
of exploring
the depths
of your own soul.

in vain,
I was asking you
to look inside your heart
and find me,

you couldn't even
find yourself.

I used
     to ache for you.
     the way
     hope
     longs to relive
     ardent moments
     buried
     under satin sheets.

now,
     I just remember you.

trying
to love you,
was like
attempting to open
my wings

and fly
underwater.

he kept bulldozing
over my heart,
until I was left
feeling nothing.
and still,
he asked me
every spring,

why I didn't smile
at the sight of
cherry blossoms.

there was a time,
when
I begged karma to hurry
and take care of you.
now,
I think
spending your life
looking for me
in every new woman you meet
and always feeling
as if you're falling short,

is going to be
punishment enough for you.

nothing,
will ever be
enough for you
after me.
you'll be chasing women
who look like me
from afar.
but when they come close,
you'll be left wanting,

as they'll never wear
the scent of my skin.

every time
you look at her,
and your heart does not want
to jump out of your chest,
as it always did before seeing me,

you'll understand
what it feels like to be settling.

forever is
a mighty long time
to spend with someone,

who doesn't know how
to light your soul on fire.

we had too much hope
and not enough trust,
in each other,
in how things would turn out.
we relied too much
on statistics, history, precedents,
and not enough on our feelings.
what if we had beat the odds?
what if it had worked out?
we wouldn't be sitting
thousands of miles apart.
we wouldn't be talking to
the moon, the sky or the stars.
instead,

we would be kissing each other good-night.

it's not that
I don't love you anymore.
I just don't think
I am strong enough,

to go through you again.

I was a wish
waiting
to become true;
if only
you had believed
in me enough.

perhaps one day,
when enough autumns,
with plenty of rain
have passed,

we will awake anew.
cleansed of the bitterness of the past,
ready to begin again.

the truth is,
I never really
wanted to forget you.
despite the pain,
I kept holding on.

until there was nothing
to hold onto anymore.

of all the lies
I've ever told my heart,
the cruelest one
was telling her
we would work out,
when

I knew we wouldn't.

nothing lasts forever.

not this pain,

not your indecision,

not my patience,

not this well of love in my heart.

- one day, it will run out.

I didn't want you to go
and now,
I don't want you
to come back
I just wish you'd stayed

...then.

you run from me.
only,
to run back to me.

we always
say good-bye
and then,
we begin again.

-not this time

The Healing

Healing starts when you decide you've had enough: enough tears have been shed; enough waves of feelings have come and gone and enough has been felt.

Sometimes we have to bury a few hopes in order to awake anew. Sometimes we wait for an *I'm sorry* that never comes, anticipating that once we receive it, all our broken pieces will reunite; and sometimes, upon receiving that I'm sorry we realize that it will never be enough to stich back together everything that has been torn inside.

Healing happens when we realize that the power to heal has always been within our reach and just waiting for us to discover it. You will find much love and forgiveness in the gentle embrace of your tears and eventually, the clouds will part and the hurricane will cease.

The seeds of healing don't start sprouting until we come back to ourselves. Within those seeds, lies a beautiful story of becoming; flowers wilt and their seeds are swallowed by the same ground they died in, only to be re-born again in something far more wondrous.

Let's not fear the falls and learn how to cherish the bruises in our hearts. Let's not dread our tears, for salt has always been a healer. Our tears merely cleansed a part of ourselves we no longer needed. And it is in this new layer of skin, of confidence, of self-love, that we can acknowledge that without breaking, we can never delve in the true depths of rebuilding.

Without succumbing to the darkness, you might have never fathomed, a strength greater than any challenge you had to face, lied dormant within you.
Because of your brokenness, you learned how to persevere, survive and flourish.

it's a daily ritual,
my re-building.
my tear-down
was gradual, too.
day by day,
brick by brick
you worked hard
to tear down my walls,
and leave me there
naked,
on the sidewalk
like a homeless woman
whose house had been taken away
from her.
stripped down
of everything I thought was mine
and left to perish
without hope.
even my soul followed you
home.

next time
someone asks you
to let go
when you are not ready,
claim your pain.
it is yours to keep
for as long as you need to,
for as long as you want to,
and no one and nothing
is entitled to taking it
away from you,
not until
you are ready to

let it go
on your own.

you're so used
to being fed empty promises,
you don't even believe
your own heart
on the days she promises
to bring you
healing.

there's this pain in your eyes,
staring back at me
no matter how much you try to hide it
behind that big smile.

let me hold space for it in my arms.
let me be the source of your light.
let me remind you that you are,

a beautiful revolution
waiting to happen.

take your heart's invitation to sadness today.
it might be anger tomorrow. pain the day after.
and all the while. trust. that it could be love.
in a week. a month. a year. your heart's walls
are coming down today. they are being burnt
down by the flames of this heartbreak. only to
rise anew soon. only this time. stronger. wiser.
more capable of love and healing.

*give your heart a chance to show you what it's
made of and allow yourself to be in awe of the
magic of its beauty and strength.*

peel off the anger,

and show me your sadness.

peel off the sadness,

and show me your pain.

peel off the pain,

and show me your love.

-let's sit here for a moment

wrap your arms
around yourself
and let yourself weep.
remember to tell your heart
this too shall pass.

there are
oceans inside of you
raging
to be heard
and felt

- listen and allow yourself to feel

just the way
you remember
to bring yourself down
for every little thing
that doesn't go
according to your plans,
don't forget
to also pat yourself on the back
every morning you wake up
and manage to leave
the comfort of your sheets
and the shelter of your home
to venture out
and face the world.

you're a priceless crystal vase,
shining brightly in the sun,
patiently waiting
for the right bouquet of roses
to adorn her interior.
but what if instead,
you *became the bouquet*
that adorned another vase
endlessly waiting to be filled
by her precious bouquet
of perfectly clipped roses?

the carriage with white lilies
and peaceful wishes
crossed the bridge of forgiveness
to make its way to you last night.

and, upon its return
I noticed, this time,
it came back to me
empty.

no hate,
no resentment,
no heaviness.
nothing, but fresh air
and freedom
in my heart.

I breathed it all in
and understood to never let go
of the power of forgiveness ever again.

tell your heart,
how proud you are of her
and how far she's come.

for no matter
how many times
she's been broken,

she has refused to harden.

so much
love
and forgiveness,
were born

in the gentle embrace
of my fragile tears.

I forgive you,
for not being able to love me,
the way I needed to be loved
for not being able to love me
the way I deserved to be loved.

I forgive,
your incapacity to give yourself to me,
the way I had given myself to you.
your reluctance to share your feelings,
according to my expectations.

I forgive you,
for the disappointment,
the heartache,
the indescribable pain you brought
onto a heart that loved you
freely and unconditionally.

for all of the above and all the ones
I do not have the strength
to pull out of myself yet,
I forgive you.
(forgiveness - part i)

I forgive myself,
for falling in love with someone
who did not see how worthy,
how valuable and how lovable I was.
for allowing my heart to feel so intensely
for someone who did not deserve
what I had to offer.
for opening up and becoming vulnerable
with someone who was not ready
to receive my vulnerability.

I forgive myself.

(forgiveness – part ii)

it is important to remember
that we are the only ones,
who hold the key
to our own peace,
calm,
and happiness
in this life.

she worried about
not being enough
for him,
without realizing that
in the process,

she had stopped
being enough
for herself.

sometimes,
the river of his memories
moves
so rapidly,
so forcefully
within me.
and I get so carried away,

I forget I can swim.

learn to love yourself,
and you will always have
a safe space
to come back to

in the middle of
life's storms.

be the wind
at your back,
blowing you
forward.

the warmest,

truest

of loves,

lies within

the confines

of your own

heart.

this crown I'm wearing,
was handed by no one.
it was not found
in an abandoned alley
one saturday morning,
while walking the dog or taking a jog.
or stumbled upon in an old attic somewhere,
waiting for me to claim it.
I've built it myself,
after having passed through many careless hands,
that left forever scars
in my soul and in my lungs.
I've breathed in doubts and swallowed lies.
I've drowned in tears and countless goodbyes.
and yet, I've risen back up,
every single time.

this crown is mine.

when I'm in need
of healing,
my written words
become fertilized soil
for the wildflower seeds
my grandmother
planted in my soul
when I was just a little girl
growing up on her farm.

center yourself into peace,
and love will come.

the kind of love
that leaves imprints
of acceptance, joy and hope.

the kind of love
you've been looking for
without ever realizing

it was always
within you.

you marvel
at the stars every night,
wondering how they find
the strength to shine in darkness
night after night.

you forget
how many times
you've dimmed your own light,
out of fear of blinding other people
with the strength
of your shine.

we are made of
so much light
that we desperately panic
whenever we see
even the slightest
rays of darkness
peeking out
of our souls.

you weren't born
to lose yourself
within this darkness.

you were born
to rise,
to shine,
and thrive.

you were born
to live,
to give,
to love,
and
to be loved.

(you're worthy and you matter)

how is it that with every day that passes by, every day that takes your hope away. as if you were invisible (not only to him, but to the world around you as well), you manage to wake up with so much love in your eyes and kindness in your heart?

how is it that every time they put you down, you not only get up, but you extend a hand to those who hurt you so they may also rise with you on those days they're down?

how is it that when you're needed, you're there for everyone, no matter how many times they fail to be there for you in your own time of need?

how is it that heartbreak softens you and invalidation strengthens you?

how is it that life works so hard at shrinking your heart and all she does is expand from all the challenges?

tonight,
pull your insecurities
from under your pillow
and burn them all
until there is nothing left,
but ashes.
then,
place lavender-scented candles
on your nightstand
and remind yourself
to breathe in the newness of life.
for every day,
is a new opportunity
to rise
and become
whom you've always known
you could be.

there is greatness
sleeping inside of you
waiting for you
to sound the alarm
and wake it up.

rise,
you, jaguar of a woman.
you, fire-breathing dragon
rise.

you were strong
before you met him.
you are strong now.

you just forgot.

(rise)

hold your knees
to your chest
hug yourself tightly
and remember:

you deserve adoration.

how about,

we take a moment to believe

that our worth

has nothing to do

with the size of our waists

and everything to do

with the size of our hearts.

tell me: how worthy do you think you are now?

the queen
inside of you,
has been patient,
she's been kind.
she's died a thousand deaths
seeing you fail yourself
over and over again
in order to please a man
not worthy of your pinky,
much less your ring finger
or the fire in your heart.
let her out of the cage
you've been holding her in
and let her remind you

of the strength
that resides
within you.

you are worth
every bit of all that love
you gave everyone else,
but never received in return.

(you could have kept it all,
but instead, you chose
to make the world feel whole)

she is in a league of her own.

she deserves to be worshipped.

she belongs on a throne,

and she doesn't even know it.

remember
that warm fall night
and the homeless man
who complimented you
on having such
a beautiful woman
on your arm?
even he knew
I was too much of a woman
for you.

I wish I had realized that, too...

now, I do.

I still wonder sometimes,

whether it was I

who loved too much,

or your hands

were just

too weak,

and too small,

to hold all the love

I so eagerly poured into

the folds of their palms.

there was
so much of you
in my heart,
there was barely
any space left
for me.

when the weight
of the world
seems to be crashing
your shoulders,
remember
that even the cape
of a superhero
can get heavy at times.

-self-care

today,
instead of carrying these mountains
on your shoulders,
big boulders of sadness, anxiety,
disappointment and sorrow,
try being the mountain yourself.

a mountain,
remains rooted and grounded
in the face of changing seasons,
storms and other weather.

exhale old perceptions of being
and seeing things.
inhale the power of
choice and transformation

and witness your life
bloom and blossom.

unleash

the power

of self-compassion

on those places

in your heart

that are still

in need of

...healing

every morning,
after you wake up,
look in the mirror
and

greet yourself
with a smile.

- befriend the eyes looking back at you.

breathe,

and the whole world

will breathe with you.

love,

and the ripples

will spread like water.

feel,

and give this world

a reason to believe there is still hope.

put your hand
over your heart,
and repeat after me:

*"I will always love myself
I will always be enough".*

always

all the women
I used to be,
bow in gratitude

to the woman
I have become.

I am
working on
being more of myself
and less of
what the world
would like me
to be.

I don't know how
to be anything else,
but whom I've become.
for I have fought long and hard
to become her.

I'm fearless.

I was tired
of hearing my story
come out of
unworthy mouths,
minimized.
when it is worth
nothing short of
being capitalized.

-on why I started writing.

The Lessons

The truth of your becoming lies hidden within your scars. There was a time when simply surviving had seemed impossible and now: wilted and torn and like a wildflower in the middle of concrete, you manage to flourish.

Stop trying to build brick homes in people who are too temporary for sandcastles. Remember that you deserve to be valued for every ounce of beauty that you so selflessly bring into this world.

Don't etch yourself clean for people who do not deserve your presence. If you do any cleaning at all, clean out your circle of friends and keep the ones who nurture your potential, rather than the ones who pressure you into living up to your potential, even on days when you need a break. Break up with your doubts and scrub yourself clean of expectations.

You don't need to ask life for permission to be whom you are dreaming of becoming. We spend way too much time looking outside of ourselves for love, validation, happiness, fulfilment, and permission to start living, without realizing that everything we need is always inside. The woman you envy, the one your soul yearns to become, is already the woman that you are.

Open your eyes to see her. Open your heart to feel her. Open your soul to welcome her in. She is perfect in her imperfection. Her vulnerability has transformed her into the most beautiful tapestry you have ever seen and she adorns your fresh.

Stop looking for light in other stars when the brightest one shines within your ribcage.

When life tries you again, learn to sing yourself to sleep with self-healing hymns that remind you of the sovereign that resides inside.

don't wish for
a love that returns.

when

you deserve
a love that stays.

life,
prepares you for notices.
you're taught to give
a two weeks' notice
when you leave your job
thirty-day notice
to find another apartment,
but hearts
don't give notices

and life
doesn't prepare your heart
for sudden goodbyes.

we live suspended
between
our past and our future,

forgetting
to enjoy our present
and all that we are now.

our eyes

hide

such

beautiful stories

of

pain,

suffering,

resilience,

hope,

and renewal

if only we looked

into each other's eyes

more often

some hope,
to one day be found
by the right person.

while others,
are on a quest
to find themselves.

-

your life
your choice

the worst things in life,
don't always come
from bad decisions.

just the way,

the best things in life,
don't always come
from good ones, either.

for some people,
you have to go to great lengths,
to picture yourself
as the perfect candidate
for their love
and they still think
you're not good enough.

while others,
can't get enough of you,
no matter how many times
you tell them about your flaws,
and everything else
you deem unlovable
about yourself.

when you,
repeatedly give your best and it is never
enough or it is taken for granted,
when you,
feel more drained than rejuvenated, around a
certain person or crowd,
when you,
need to explain yourself
a little too often and a little too much,

it is not the time to wonder
whether you are doing something wrong.

it is the right time to
realize that
you are hanging around
the wrong crowd.

there are those,
who are impatient
with your healing and growing.
constantly putting pressure on you to live up
to your potential.

and then there are those,

who introduce you to your potential,
when you can't even see it yourself.

when someone
talks a certain way about you,
ask yourself,
how much of what they're saying
is about you,

and how much of it,
is about themselves.

there are mouths,
that melt our insecurities
and make us open
more than just our thighs.
and then,
there are those
that melt our self-esteem
to the point of
ending up wondering
if we were ever worth anything.

*(kiss a mouth that opens up your soul,
instead of one that tears it up)*

we look at our scars

and fear

that anyone

who catches a glimpse of them might be

tempted to

look the other way

instead of seeing them

as the blessings that they are

for pruning away

all the cowards

who would have fled

with their tails between their legs

at the very first sight

of our depth, anyway.

see, the trouble was:
you failed to see me – as I was
and not as you wanted me to be.

and all I ever really wanted,
was for you to see me
in all the glory of my complexity.

what I tell you
about myself,
has nothing to do
with how you interpret
my words.
I can tell you
that I see myself
as a *beautiful deer,*
sprinting freely
through the thick forest,
and you can then tell me
that *I'm prey.*

we shrink. we shrink ourselves. we shrink our dreams.

we abandon our visions of expansion to make others feel comfortable around us. we hide our growth when we feel that it might intimidate someone close to us. we hide our happiness when life smiles back at us not to feel guilty about the suffering of others. we become words, when we were meant to be stories. we become dots of light at the end of tunnels, when we have stars waiting to burst out of our chests and illuminate the world. we conform. we settle.

and we die with regret throwing punches between our ribs, demanding to know why we stood by and did nothing while there was still time.

no,
this fancy new watch
is not going to be able to
buy you back
all the time you lost
thinking you were pursuing
what was important,
when in reality,

you were giving up the meaningful
to chase the meaningless.

don't dive into
the fast-flowing
waters of love,
with the expectation
of making it
to the other side
without a scratch.

love,
can kill distance;

the same way that

distance,
can kill love.

I have loved
the most
ordinary of men,
with
the most
extraordinary of passions.

we love,

the most deserving of men
in the most undeserving of ways.
and the most undeserving of men
in the most deserving of fashions.

and that's where we go wrong.

some days,

the woman in front of you,

doesn't need you

to solve her problems

or for you to bring her smile

back from the dead.

some days,

all she needs is

to be listened to,

to be seen,

to be heard

and to be understood.

-a message for the men in our lives

she deserves
the wholeness of you
no half-measures here.
you are not making a cake,
you're loving a woman,
a goddess,
a wild spirit,
a tornado,
an ocean too deep and complex,
for you to ever get
to the bottom of.

it is not enough to tell her
that you love her.

your words,
have to come
from a place of true love
and adoration.

women,
crave the kind of love
that makes them feel

not only desired,
but also secure.

refuse to be
someone's midnight snack.
you deserve
to be savored
slowly
and mindfully
by his soul,
not quickly
and mindlessly
by his body.

while your ears
spend precious moments
craving the I love you's
his lips refuse to utter,
there is another
dreaming of all the ones

you keep prisoners
on the tip of your tongue.

don't let his incertitude
pour false hope
into your soul.

you deserve a love
that wants to be by your side.
you have no need for
a love that is still questioning
whether you are worth it to love.

you are.

always have been.

always will be.

and in all your beauty,
your rawness and vulnerability,

you are too much of a woman
for boys still figuring out
how to be men.

some of us,

have all the reasons in the world to leave,

and yet, we choose to hold on and try again.

while others,

have plenty of reasons to stay,

and yet, they choose to give up

and walk away.

the wrong man
will always find
reasons to leave.

while,

the right man
will always find
enough reasons to stay.

the longer
the good-bye,
the harder it is
to let go.

you sit around,
waiting for him to realize
how good of a catch you were,
instead of you realizing,

how much better you can do now
with him out of the picture.

you're tired
of fighting for someone
who will not fight for you.

you're exhausted
from finding excuses
to behaviors that should not be excused.

you pray
to find someone who could see
that you are worth fighting for.

but darling,
the brave heart that you're looking for
won't be found hidden in cowards,
but in dreamers.

all this time,

you've been looking for love
in all the wrong places.

sometimes, we are in love with a memory, an experience, a fantasy, a dream, a hope. we suffer, believing we are in love with a person, when in fact, we are in love with the idea of love and the person just happens to walk by while we are daydreaming about an idealized love.

I think I fell
for whom I remembered you to be.
and not for who you were
in your bones,
and beneath your skin.
I fell for a soul
that was born out of my soul.
no wonder,

you always felt
so much like home.

I spent years
thinking
I had lost you.
when in reality,
you
were the one who
lost me.

and then,
she decided it was time
she stopped wishing her life away
wishing for him.

you're not
the man I love, anymore.

you're just
a man I used to know.

no one knows you better than
your own heart.

and yet,

you continue to look for answers in all
these other hearts.

I had wrongly assumed that
closure comes with walking away
when in fact,

closure comes, the moment you find
a good enough reason to stay away.

-walking away is easy;
staying away is the hard part

it was
in my moment of need,
where I discovered
your truest self.

it was
in your silence,
where I found
my closure.

closure,

doesn't leave the door ajar
in case he decides to come back.

closure,

doesn't leave space for maybes
and doesn't look back.

closure,

invites new opportunities
with someone who deserves you,
who honors the specialness of your heart,
who showers you with attention and love,
and acknowledges that,

you are worth all of that and more!

the real issue

with people who leave,

is that

they never stay gone.

they pop up into your life again,

right when

you were finally,

ready to move on –

as if

somehow,

they felt you slipping

from under their grip

and wanted to see,

if they could

pull you back in,

just for fun.

we used up
all the words to
tear each other apart
and now,

there are none left
to bring us back together.

when
you feel broken,
there is no safer place to be in
than the sanctuary
of your own heart.

on the other side
of every goodbye,
there is a hello
patiently waiting
its turn.

-welcome it in

spring doesn't give up on flowers when she sees them sleeping in winter. never give up on love, no matter how hard it feels to keep holding onto hope. one day, the love you're looking for will meet you out of nowhere. it will not ask questions. it will not make demands. it will fall. effortlessly. into your arms. and want you to cradle it. nourish it. feed it, everything you had been carrying inside for so long. too long. forever.

and you will finally
feel free. weightless. but
oh, so full.
so bountiful.

sealing off your heart
won't prevent people
from hurting you.
it will only prevent you
from living
a life full of love.

don't wait
until you lose her,
to decide you want to love her.

love her
while you still can,
so you never have to lose her.

we hold on,
when we should be
letting go.
and we let go,
when we should be holding on
with everything we have and more.

and that's how we learn.

too many times
we say goodbye,
when in reality
all we wish
we could say is:
please, stay.

don't let

fear

steal

true love

away from you.

don't allow yourself

to one day

wake up

to a stranger

you never wanted

in your bed

in the first place.

don't settle.

formatting

we have gotten into the habit of formatting
everything. we don't just stop at formatting
lines on a screen to please the eye anymore.
we format the words that come out of our
mouths, so the people in our lives will love and
appreciate us enough not to leave.

we format the décor of our houses and the
look of our food to fit into the box of what is
considered beautiful, healthy, and acceptable.
we format our dreams to fit a mold accepted
by a society that is constantly judging every
move we make, eagerly waiting for us to fail at
something, no matter how small.

we format our bodies to look as close as
possible to what the magazines force-feed us
to believe is attractive. the clothes we wear,
the lives we lead, even the way we love is
programmed into us to fit societal molds.

we live entire lives meant to please other
people and only remember the importance of
pleasing our souls when the end is near and
there is not much left to do anymore. we grow

up trying to please our parents, then move into trying to please our partners, our friends and our children, forgetting to please the most important person in our lives: our inner child. no wonder we feel more dead than alive on most days.

our entire existence is spent looking for new ways of formatting ourselves to fit into new boxes. we ignore the screams of our souls, when they have had enough and want to break free, because the pull to remain the same. to fit in. is stronger than the push to change and become visionaries in a world forcing us to stay the same.

we were born to stand out,
yet every day, we fight to fit in. we need to
break the cycle of conformity and

choose to stand out.

if we can't
be alone sometimes,
we can't successfully be together
with anyone.

the secret
to becoming better
at loving, is

to start by practicing
loving yourself first.

for every moment,
you couldn't love her,

you taught her,
she could love herself.

maybe my heart
did weigh a lot more
when in pieces.
all of a sudden,
I feel so much lighter.

and that's how I know,
I've now let you go.

I stopped trying to be
whom I thought
he would love,
the moment I realized
that by loving myself
I would become

the one
he wouldn't be able
to live without.

a woman
who values herself,
who appreciates the beauty of her dreams,
who believes in the strength of her spirit,
who enjoys time alone,
who knows how to water her own seeds of
growth and healing,
who sets healthy boundaries in love and
friendships,
who carries an unlimited amount of hope and
goodness in her heart,
who turns heartbreak and sadness into
lessons,
who doesn't give up when everything around her
is telling her that she should,

*that's one special woman to watch out for and hold
on to.*
*for she will let you know when she feels taken for
granted,*
*but also bring magic into your life when she feels
seen, loved and cherished.*

you,
my love,
are a queen.

you,
are not
an object to be used
or experimented with.

you,
are not
an outfit to be put on
when lust strikes him.

you,
are to be
loved and accepted
in all your uniqueness and complexity.

it takes time
to start believing in yourself again.
after years of staying on the accepted path,
it is normal to be afraid or hesitant
to head in your own direction.
there is no failure in safety,
but there is also no success.
slowly, trust your heart
and believe that the ability
to attain whatever you seek
rests dormant within you.
give your imagination the power
to set your talents free.
give yourself the chance to discover
that dreams do come true.
nurture that hope
and there will be nothing
you won't be able to achieve.

there comes a point in your life when you have to realize that standing still no longer serves you. change can be frightening and challenging yourself into letting go of old patterns of thought and behavior can seem impossible at times. listening to those who ridicule the choices you make, the roads you have chosen to travel, and the chances you have taken, might seem inescapable at first. there will always be those who try to steal the shine in your eyes with their laughter and criticism. those are the ones who tend to judge a vision they do not yet understand.

but the more you surround yourself with people who share your vision of the future, who believe in you and who will help keep your dream alive, the more you will learn to be less afraid of making mistakes and to be more focused on finding the route that works best for you. it is only through taking the risks that others fear that you can achieve greatness. keep your belief in yourself as you venture into this new journey and take your time with it.

you are never too late, or too early. you are always just on time to embrace the spectacular beauty of your future.

one day,

all the effort,

the love

and

all the second chances

you've given others

(time and time again)

will find their way back to you.

and when they do,

they'll hug you so tight,

they'll never want

to let go

of your warmth

ever again.

(I promise)

inside all of us,
there's a flower
waiting for
the right time

to bloom.

there is always,
always
still
plenty of time
to bloom.

(always)

my dear reader,

inhale forgiveness
exhale resentment
inhale freedom
exhale entrapment

inhale self-compassion
exhale judgment
inhale healing
exhale suffering

inhale renewal
exhale pain

may you be free
to love again.

Final Note

Somehow, you have made it to the end of the book! Thank you for being tender with my heart and using kind eyes when reading my story! It is my sincere hope that this book has brought some shred of hope into your heart and that it will be useful to you in enhancing the quality of your life and relationships. My hope is that both women and men benefit from it.

Sometimes men forget how important it is for a woman to have her emotional needs met above all; they forget that while we all yearn connection, women especially, seem to thrive on it when it is given to them in abundance. It is understandable why one could be afraid of voicing feelings out of fear of being laughed at or scolded for not saying the "right" thing. However, I hope this book gave you a glimpse into how hurtful disconnection can be to a woman's heart.

There are many things that could go wrong when you speak your mind, but there are also many that could potentially go right. *I hope you choose to take responsibility for your feelings and show the woman you love how you truly feel, instead of having her guess your intentions and let her make assumptions. I hope you decide to be more courageous and open with the special women in your lives. There is so much magic waiting for you on the other side of vulnerability.* Don't be scared to go there! Don't be scared to open that sacred door that holds so many secret rooms you'd never otherwise be able to access. When you close yourself off to things, things also close off to you! I wish you strength and courage in your pursuit of love and if you've been hurt: I wish you healing.

To the women who have honored me with taking the time to read this book: *I hope it was not wasted time. I hope this book encouraged you to recognize the worthiness of your heart and the value of your love; I hope it inspired you to re-evaluate your standards, and to make the decision not to continue a pattern of hurt and settling for less than what you deserve! You deserve a waterfall kind of love: always flowing...pouring itself for you...cascading in layers of admiration, support and never-ending passion.*

In life, you will get only what you seek! My final hope for you my reader...is that you choose to seek love; that you choose to seek acceptance; that you choose to seek gratitude and forgiveness; and above all...I hope you decide to choose YOU! Choose to honor and respect your heart every day; choose to lead with your soul more than with your thoughts and choose to FEEL, even when life proves difficult!

If you have to drown in something, drown in self-love and self-appreciation while you strip your soul naked of people's opinions of you; the only opinion that should truly matter in this life is your own! Soak in your truth and let go of the desire or the inclination to try and persuade the world of your worth!

From my heart to
yours...I wish you
LOVE and HEALING!

Epilogue

It was when I stopped caring about the inconsequential aspects of life, that I finally began to step out from beneath my old skin and feel that I began to live. It was when I realized that life was not meant to be lived satisfying others, while asking the unachievable out of myself that magic started happening.

Life flows through us at such a rapid pace! Time does not wait for anyone to take steps towards accomplishing dreams or figuring out what gives meaning and purpose to their lives; time does not forgive when you take forever to tell that special someone you love them. There is no better time to do all the things you wanted to do than today, for tomorrow is not guaranteed to anyone.

I've learned to live each day in deep gratitude. There are people who did not get to wake up this morning. There are people who will not get to tuck their kids into bed this evening or kiss them good-night. There are many who take their final breaths as my hands touch these keys. There are many praying for just a few more hours, minutes, seconds on this Earth to get one last good look at everything they love and wish they would not have to leave behind. As I'm writing this and you are reading it: we are both blessed to be alive!

My journey of reshaping has been anything but

easy, yet I can't help but hold my becoming in deep gratitude as without this journey, I would have been stuck in a mind and a heart I did not recognize as my own. I've changed. I have become so many other women in this process. *And most of these women, I've slipped off as dresses that I once loved, but that did not fit me anymore.* I've traveled so many miles inside this tired mind of mine. I've discovered places in my heart I never knew existed; I've explored my darkness and conquered my fears.

Humans have a tendency to remain complacent in the known, unhappy, but still in the known; instead of venturing out and exploring what lies beyond their comfort zone. Humans settle for the sake of safety. I got tired of settling, of slow-dancing with the idea of letting go of my old self and my old patterns of behavior. I wanted to never stop growing. In the busyness of our lives, we constantly try to speed everything up and find quick fixes. But, for some things, there are no quick fixes. There is no easy way of letting go; there are no shortcuts and no magic pills that could make some feelings go away. It is easy to wish for them to go away, but in reality, they are all gifts, wrapped a little differently than you might have expected. And any attempt to put pressure on yourself to speed up the process of taking in the meaning of these gifts, will only make them stay longer and hurt deeper. I learned that I need to sit with them and get comfortable in the unknown, in the uncomfortable...until I learn what I was meant to learn and then, I can move forward. It is in busyness and outside noise where dreams, hopes and feelings go to die. It is in quietude that nurture, healing and growth are given a second chance to be re-born.

When we sit with our sadness, our brokenness, our worry; when we befriend what is troubling us, it all starts to seem less scary and more manageable. There will be many beautiful beginnings born from painful endings and there will be much strength born from forgiveness and acceptance of self. I've learned to appreciate all that I am and the beauty of my flaws much like a Kintsugi artist looking at his beautiful pieces of pottery before bringing out the gold and attaching the broken pieces back together.

I am my flaws. I am my feelings. I am my fragments. I owned my story. I owned my truth. I am gold. I am unbreakable and ever-changing,

as every time I break, every time I fall apart, I become more and more of whom I was meant to be. I am everything I need and I am enough. I have always been enough...*and now, I know it.*

The Acknowledgements

This book would not have been possible without the talent, love, care and support of the following people:

• *This book would not have existed without my grandmother, Ioana.* She raised me a fighter and a survivor and I owe everything I am in this life to her. This is not my accomplishment: this is our accomplishment! You could have written this book yourself, if you had not given up your life to raise me...and for that...I will never find the right words to express my gratitude. *Te iubesc si imi e dor de tine...in fiecare zi...Desi esti departe..te simt mereu langa mine...*

• *A huge thank you to my husband* for giving me free-reign when it came to what I could write about; for enabling me to live my dream of writing; for putting up with my many moody nights of relentless editing; for being my shoulder to cry on when memories of the past were too much to take in and when self-doubt knocked on my door to tempt me with not publishing the book after all, because no one was going to read it anyway. *Thank you for being there for me: I love you!*

• *My heartfelt thanks to my best friends Irina and Anda!* Neither one of you is romantic or much into poetry, and yet...you never complained about me sending you my very first pieces of writing and asking you to give your opinion. Thank you for keeping it real for me and letting me know when things seemed too much or too little for you. Thank you for pushing me to continue, every time I stopped to ponder whether I should go through with this or not. *I love, love, love you both so much and I know I should tell you this more often!*

• *I have been blessed to receive guidance and support from my friends: Marni Dieanu, Iulia Poenaru, Nicoleta Casangiu, Dana Coman and Katy Scott* who are all spread out around the world, but who never cease to amaze me with the kindness of their hearts: I always feel you so close to me!!! Thank you all for the insightful comments! You ladies have been such pillars on this journey! You literally believed in me and my book more than I believed in myself!!! *I adore you and am forever grateful to have friends like you in this life!!!*

• *My immense love and appreciation to Gloria Truong and Nadia Nader* who read and re-read my work and no matter how tired or busy they were, they made time to give me constructive feedback and tell me I should continue this journey! Thank you for offering me a safe space to share my feelings when they became too much and for always having a way to keep hope alive in my heart. *I am so grateful that life has brought us together! I value our friendship so much!*

- *My deepest gratitude to Beatriz Mutelet* for the cover and interior illustrations. Thank you for lending your talent to make this book exactly what I envisioned! *Thank you for adding that much needed magical touch to such a sacred piece of my heart!*

- *Thank you, Mitch Green* for the beautiful cover design and interior formatting of the book! Your patience and professionalism are highly appreciated!! The layout is stunning and you went above and beyond to brainstorm ideas and answer my questions and make the process of helping me with publishing my first book as seamless as possible.

- *My infinite thanks to Ruby Dhal* for being such a big supporter on this journey and for so graciously offering to write the most heartfelt review of the book. Thank you for listening to me complaining and for putting my doubts to sleep when they were louder than my dreams. Thank you for not getting tired of me and not giving up!!! And, thank you for being such an inspiration! *I appreciate you more than you will ever know!*

- *Thank you to Molly Hillery* for giving me hope every time it seemed to slip away; for the many conversations we shared on so many topics ranging from mental health advocacy to personal struggles along our writing journeys.

Thank you for believing in this book enough to want to put your name on its back cover. *I don't know how I stumbled upon you, Molly... but somehow the Universe seemed to believe I needed you in my life...Thank you for responding to my heart's calling!*

• *To A for the story and the lessons. I hope you find love in worthy arms and I hope it is exactly what you've been hoping for your life!*

• *And last, but definitely not least, a very special thank you to you, my dedicated reader...* You cannot imagine the joy it gives me that somehow this book found a home in your hands! Your unwavering support and kind words inspire me every day! I never in my wildest dreams would have thought that I'd be here today, writing for such a huge following on social media.

Thank you for believing in me
enough to give me a chance to
share my story with you! Thank y
ou for taking a walk through the
garden of my thoughts and feelings...
I hope you found a shred of hope
and healing...if not in my lines...
maybe between them. THANK YOU!

About The Author

Madalina is a writer, poet, mother, wife, and an aspiring psychologist. Madalina has always been a lover of books, words and creative expression. Originally from Romania, Madalina has published extensively in Romanian, but this is her first publication in English. She speaks several languages and credits writing with having helped her get through some of the hardest times of her life.

She is currently working as a therapist trainee in Northern California while finishing a Master in Counseling Psychology and preparing to apply to Doctoral Programs upon graduation. She finds joy in working with children (as she appreciates their genuineness and lack of layers), as well as working with couples (as she has always been intrigued by the dynamics that make some couple break apart and others thrive).

When she is not writing, doing therapy or going to school, Madalina is busy researching ways to advocate for mental health and to eliminate the stigma that is often associated with mental illness. She enjoys writing about love, heartbreak, grief, healing, self-compassion, self-acceptance and self-care.

At the moment, Madalina is working on her second collection of poetry.

You can find Madalina on
Instagram: www.instagram.com/madalinacoman
Facebook: www.facebook.com/madalina.poetry

Twitter: www.twitter.com/mada_c